SIMPLE TECHNOLOGY

INCLINES

Liz Lennon and Ellie O'Shea

WINDMILL BOOKS

Published in 2026 by Windmill Books,
an Imprint of Rosen Publishing
2544 Clinton St.
Buffalo, NY 14224

First published in Great Britain in 2023 by Wayland

Editor: Sarah Peutrill
Designer: Lisa Peacock
Science consultant: Peter Riley

Cataloging-in-Publication Data
Names: Lennon, Liz, author. | O'Shea, Ellie, illustrator.
Title: Inclines / by Liz Lennon, illustrated by Ellie O'Shea.
Description: Buffalo, NY : Windmill Books, 2026. | Series: Simple technology | Includes glossary and index.
Identifiers: ISBN 9781725397101 (pbk.) | ISBN 9781725397118 (library bound) | ISBN 9781725397125 (ebook)
Subjects: LCSH: Inclined planes--Juvenile literature.
Classification: LCC TJ1428.L46 2026 | DDC 621.8--dc23

Printed in China

CPSIA Compliance Information: Batch #QW26WM
For Further Information contact Rosen Publishing at 1-800-237-9932

CONTENTS

WHAT IS AN INCLINE?

Have you ever whooshed down a slide or pushed a toy car up a ramp? These are both kinds of inclined plane, or incline.

There are different sorts of incline, and they can help us in different ways.

What different inclines have in common is that they are all simple machines!

Inclines are sometimes called ramps or slopes.

EFFORT AND INCLINE

Imagine you have to lift a heavy box into the back of a truck. Holding it up is hard! It's easier to walk up a ramp with it.

Moving the box up a slope takes less effort or force than lifting it straight up.

GENTLE OR STEEP?

An incline can be gentle or steep. Think about when you walk up a steep path up a hill. It's harder work than walking up a gentle, winding path.

Look at these two ramps.
What do you notice?

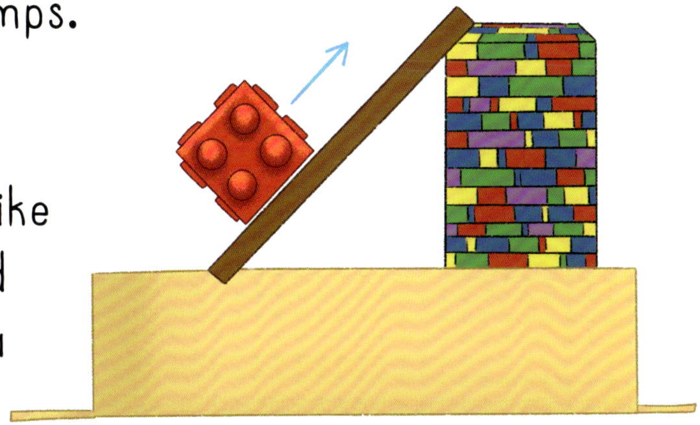

This ramp is steep. Like the hill path, it's hard work to push or pull a box up this slope.

This incline is gentler. It is easier to push or pull a box up this slope. But there is further to go.

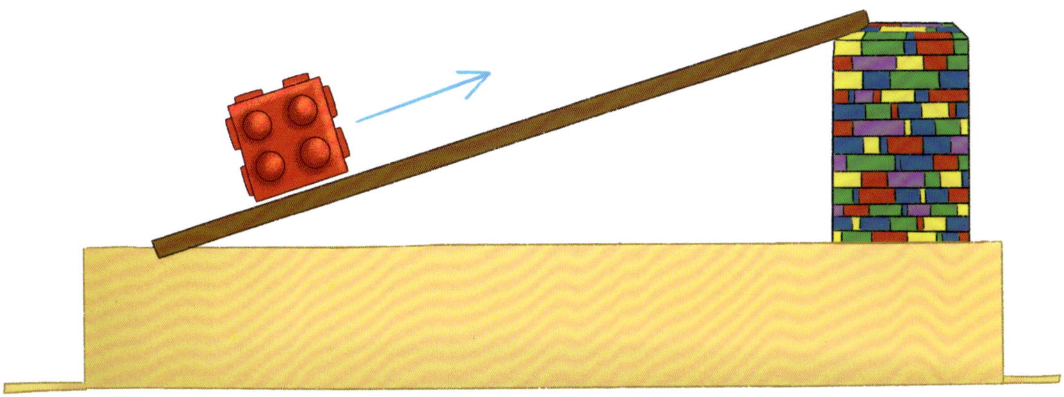

GOING DOWN

In the same way that slopes help us move things upward, they also help us move downward.

This ski slope is a ramp for skiing down.

It takes very little effort to get to the bottom.

You do need a little skill however!

SLOPE EXPERIMENT

Jaz has rested a plank on a building block. She lets a toy car travel down her ramp and measures how far it goes.

Now she adds another block on top of the first. This time, the car travels faster and further.

You could try this experiment too.

USEFUL SLOPES

These slopes are useful.

This ramp helps people who can't use the stairs.

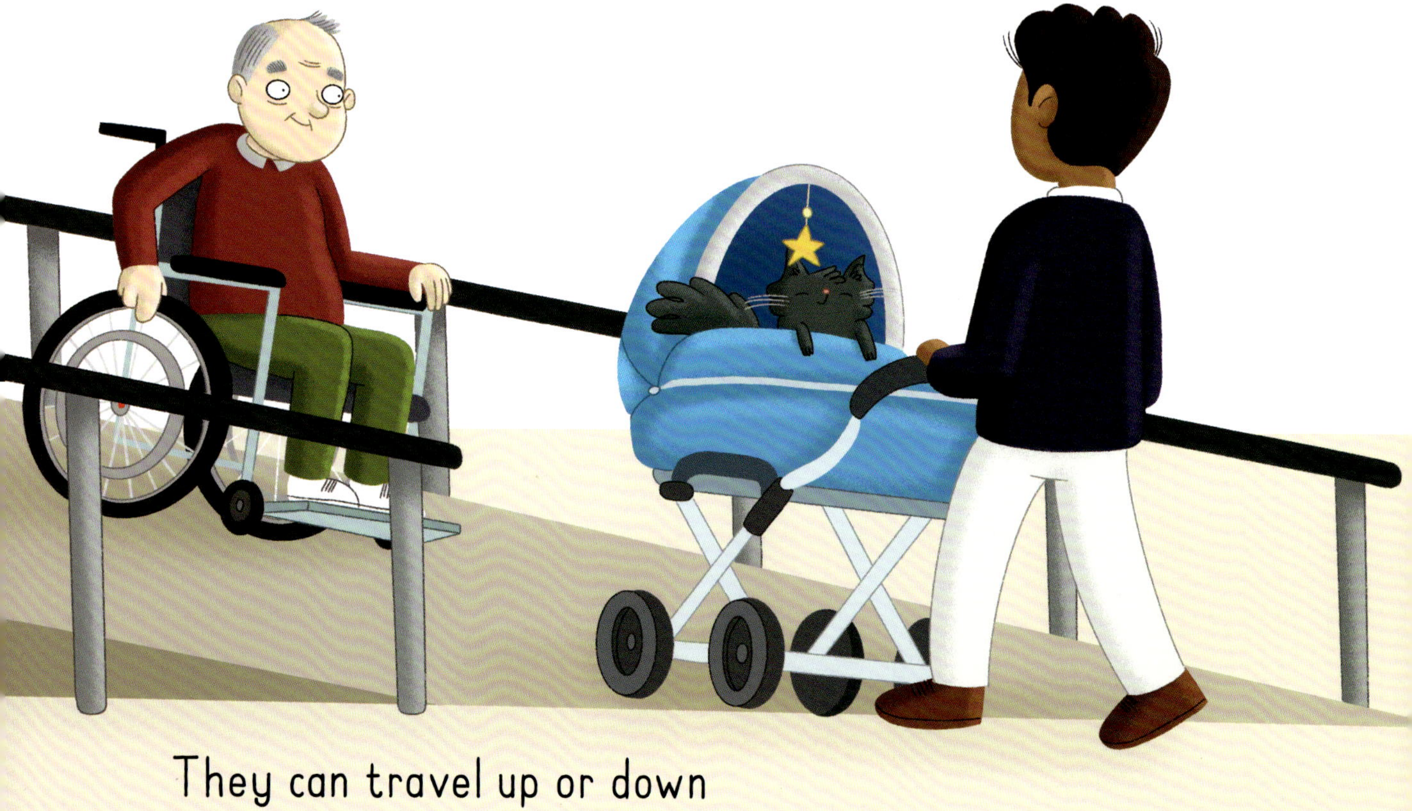

They can travel up or down the ramp.

This ramp helps people lift heavy loads on to the shelf.

FUN SLOPES

These slopes are for fun! They are different kinds of slide. Which one is your favorite?

Waterslide

Playground slide

Spiral slide

SCREWS

A screw is similar to a nail, but it has a winding ridge, a kind of incline around it. This is called a thread.

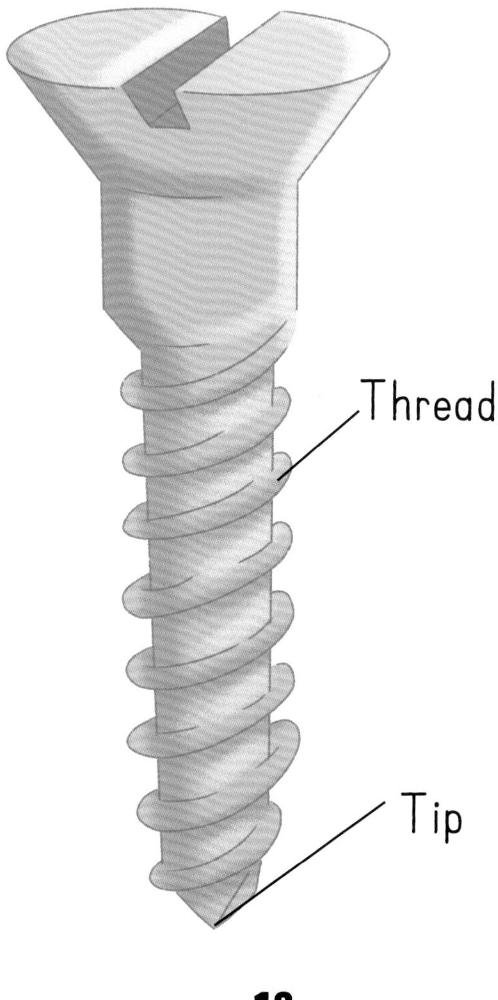

When you turn a screw, the thread travels a long way. It goes round and round and the tip of the screw goes in a little bit at a time.

It takes less effort or force to turn a screw than to push a nail straight in.

USING SCREWS

A screw is useful for holding things together, such as two pieces of wood.

Some light bulbs have a screw to keep them in place.

Even bottle caps are a kind of screw!

You twist the cap to easily remove it.

Next time you have a bottle of water, take a look inside and you'll see the inclined plane twisting around!

WEDGES

A wedge is a simple machine made up of two inclined planes. These planes meet and form a sharp edge.

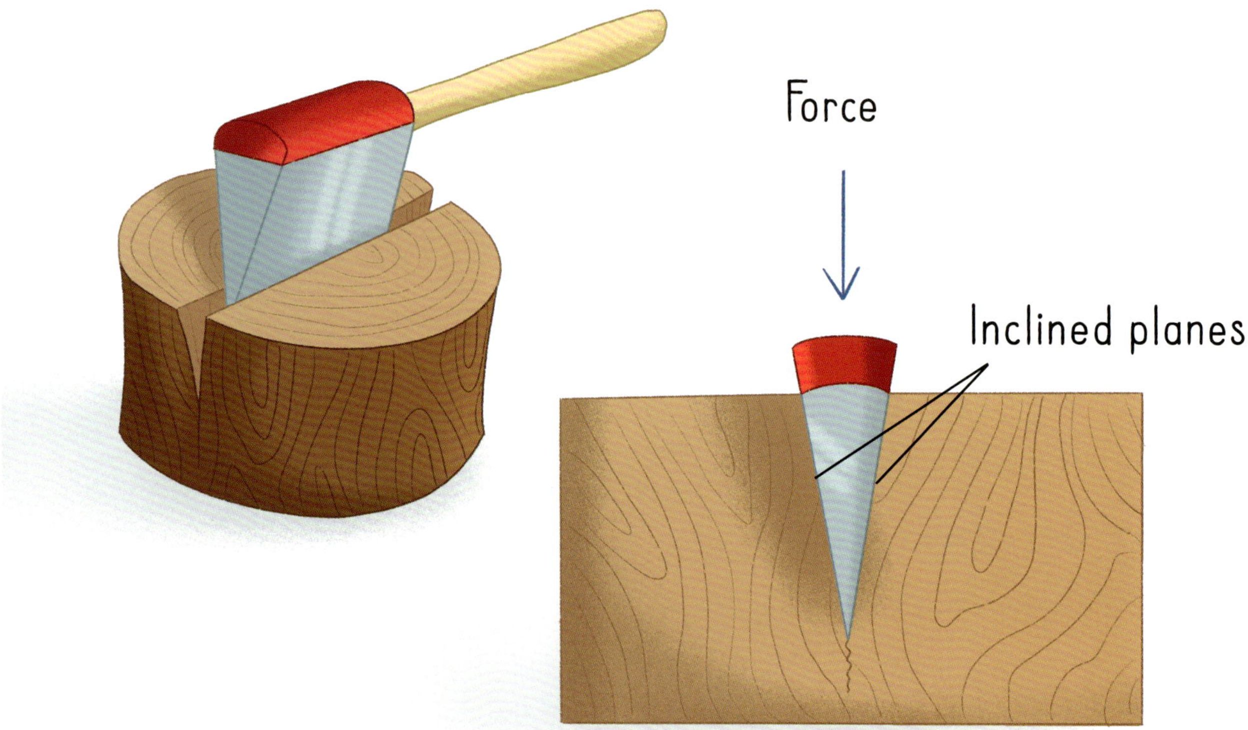

This ax is a wedge. The wedge works by changing the direction of the force. When a person swings an ax, the force is moving in the direction of the swing.

When the ax hits the trunk, the force can suddenly not move in the same direction. Instead, the force goes to the sides of the wedge.

Knives are also wedges. Max is using a knife to split apart an orange.

DOORSTOPPER

A doorstopper is another kind of wedge. You use one to keep a door open.

The doorstopper changes the direction of the force. Unlike the ax or knife though, this wedge is not splitting things apart.

WEDGES IN NATURE

Although we make lots of machines that are wedges, we can also find wedges in nature.

A woodpecker's beak is a type of wedge when it pecks at a tree.

Your front teeth are wedges when they cut through your food.

INCLINES IN THE PAST

Inclined planes have been used by people for thousands of years to move heavy objects.

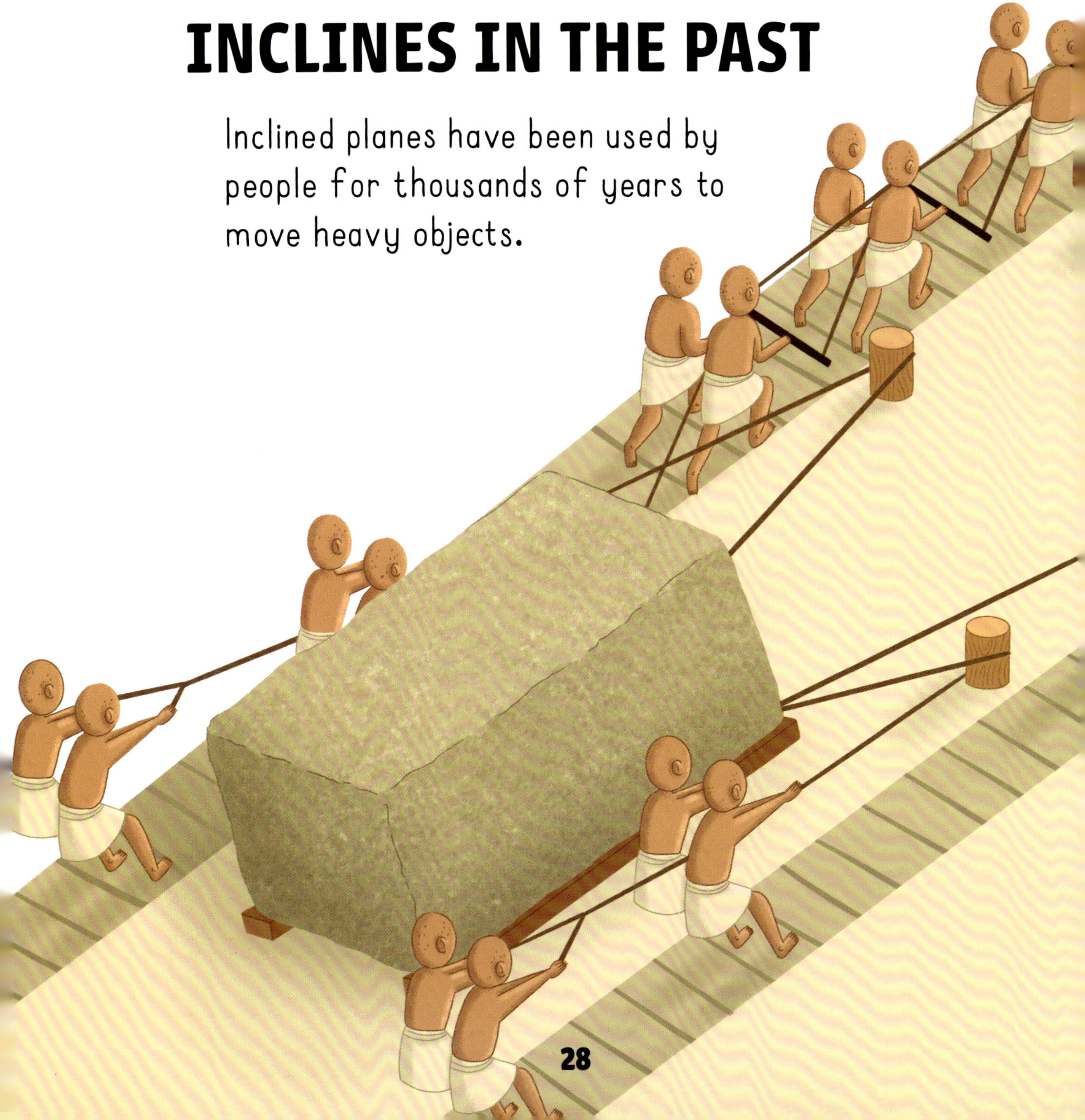

In ancient Egypt, wedges were used to break away blocks of rock used for building.

GLOSSARY

Here are the key words we explored in this book. Try covering the meanings to see if you can remember them yourself. Were you right?

Ax a kind of wedge that is used for splitting things apart.

Effort a push or a pull.

Force a push or a pull.

Inclined plane another name for a slope.

Load this is the something that has to be moved from one place to another, such as a heavy box.

Machine anything that helps us by taking a force and transferring it to where it is needed.

Ramp another name for a slope.

Screw a metal or plastic stick with a twisty, ridged slope around it used to hold things together. When you turn a screw with a screwdriver, the slope catches onto the material you're screwing it into, and pulls the screw in.

Wedge something such as an ax, a beak, or a doorstopper, which has two slopes that come together to a point.

INDEX